D0574352

Animal **Snacks**

Dawn Cusick

EarlyLight Books

Waynesville, North Carolina, USA

Design: Stewart Pack
Photo Research: Beth Fielding
Copy Editor: Karen Backstein

10 9 8 7 6 5 4 3 2 1

First edition

Published by EarlyLight Books, Inc.
1436 Dellwood Road, Waynesville, NC 28786, USA

ISBN-13: 978-0-9832014-5-8

Library of Congress Control Number: 2012939650

Contents

Animal Snacks

All animals in the Kingdom Animalia, from spiders to snails to snakes, ingest their food. They can't make their own food, the way plants do, or absorb their food, the way fungi do. Animal foods are broken down inside their bodies into small pieces (molecules) used to make the chemical energy animals need to live.

Camouflage

Many types of animals, including this stink bug, hide from predators with body colors that match their food.

Learn more about otter diets on page 40.

Food Chains

Food chains tell us what animals are eating in specific places. Some biologists study the world's food chain; others study food chains in smaller places, such as a lake or a dessert. All of the animals in this book are **consumers** in their food chains. This means they are eating plants, fungi, bacteria, protists, or other animals.

Other types of living organisms in food chains are **producers** such as plants and some bacteria that use energy from the sun to make their own food. Food chains also have **decomposers** such as bacteria and fungi that break down dead plants and animals into small molecules or atoms that can be recycled by other organisms.

Some animals are **specialists**, eating just one type of food. Other animals are **generalists**, eating many types of food. What are you? A specialist or a generalist?

In every food chain there are **predators** (the hunters) and **prey** (the animals being hunted). Predators hunt for prey in many ways. Sit-and-wait predators find a good hiding place and wait quietly for prey to pass by. In contrast, some predators are fast runners, flyers, or swimmers, and chase down their prey.

Prey animals have many **adaptations** to avoid being eaten. Some have colors and patterns that help them blend in (camouflage) with their environment. Others have bright colors that warn predators they will taste bad, or venom or spines to protect themselves. Still others protect themselves by staying in large groups.

Bird Snacks

There are almost 10,000 species of birds, and many of them eat just one type of food such as nectar, seeds, nuts, insects, fish, snakes, or carrion (dead animals). A bird's beak usually gives good clues about what types of foods the bird eats. Long, thin beaks, such as the hummingbird's beak, help get nectar from deep inside flowers. Parrot beaks are short and strong, while owl and vulture beaks have sharp hooks for tearing flesh.

Sweet Treats

Hummingbirds move their long, hollow tongues through their beaks to suck out sweet plant nectar.

Opposite page, clockwise from top left: A black-cheeked woodpecker eating fruit, a European goldfinch eating thistle seeds, a parrot feeding on an almond, and a cedar waxwing eating berries.

Bird Snacks

Birds can eat a lot of caterpillars and other types of larvae. In one experiment, biologists found that when there were more caterpillar-eating birds in a forest, some types of trees had healthier leaves. Why would this be? The caterpillars eat leaves, and when there were fewer caterpillars, the trees had many more leaves!

Baby Food

A pair of Eastern bluebirds with food for their nestlings.

Above: Three nestlings beg for the same insect. Which one will get the treat?

Above, right: A parrot gets a drink from a bird bath.

Right: A penguin eats snow.

Below: Young goslings search the ground for insects.

Bird Snacks

Many large African mammals such as the African buffalo, the impala, the hippo, the zebra, and the giraffe have a close relationship with birds called a **symbiosis**. The birds eat insects, ticks, and leeches from the animals' skin. For more examples of mutualism involving food, see pages 32 and 33 to learn about cleaner fish.

Movable Feasts

Left and below: Red-billed oxpecker birds clean the fur and skin of an African buffalo and an impala.

Right-hand page: Cattle egrets use the backs of hippopotamuses as a safe place to search for fish. While they wait, they also eat ticks and leeches.

**Put Your Eye
On the Prize**

Nestling Snacks

Newborn birds (called hatchlings) drink special "milk" given to them by their parents. After a few days, the young birds are called nestlings and are fed insects, berries, fish, or meat. The insides of baby bird mouths are often brightly colored, which may help them remind their parents to feed them when they beg with their mouths open.

Open Wide!

Left and above: A male tree swallow gives food to a nestling. Both male and female adults catch flying insects such as grasshoppers and beetles, then bring them back to the nest to feed their young birds.

Weak Beaks

Young birds
cannot hold
their own food
so their parents
drop it into
their mouths.

Bird Snacks

Everyone knows that snakes eat a lot of bird eggs and hatchlings, but did you know that some birds eat a lot of snakes? Their beaks, feathers, and scales offer some protection from snake bites, but catching snakes still requires patience and skill. The stork below may need to pick up and drop the snake many times before it dies and can be eaten. In many places, storks are loved as a snake-killing symbol.

Hold on Tight!

Snake snackers

How do birds catch snakes? If the question were a joke, we would answer, "Very carefully." It's not a joke, though. Flying takes a lot of energy, and birds that do not eat enough food do not live long. When catching snakes, some birds (such as the owl at left or the heron below left) use their beaks to cut off the snake's air supply, while other birds (such as the eagle below right) stand on top of the snake. The secretary bird from Africa (right) kills snakes by kicking them!

Bird Snacks

How do birds find their food? Well, it depends on the kind of bird and the type of food! Some birds look for a special shape, while others sit and wait, watching for their prey to move. Other birds find food with their sense of smell. Still other birds, such as woodpeckers, use their sense of touch to feel vibrations made by insects living inside trees.

Dinner?

Turkey vultures are scavengers. They use their good eyesight and strong sense of smell to find dead animals.

Stop, Thief!

Below, a crow is caught with a rooster's foot in its mouth! Crows can fly as far as 50 miles a day searching for food. They are opportunistic omnivores, which means they eat whatever they find.

Frog feasts

It's a good thing female frogs lay thousands of eggs because many animals prey on frogs. Here, a yellowbilled hornbill (left), a great white egret (right), and a Taiwan whistling thrush (below) all eat frogs.

Streamside Hunting

The Taiwan whistling thrush hunts on rocks near streams, where it finds lizards, snakes, frogs, crabs, worms, and insects.

Bird Snacks

Birds that live near water are good at catching fish and other animals that live in or near streams, rivers, ponds, lakes, and oceans. A bird that specializes in eating slow-moving animals such as caterpillars would have trouble catching fast-moving animals such as fish!

Meow

Catfish use their long, whisker-like barbels to find their food, while herons use their long, thin beaks to pluck catfish out of the water.

Catch of the Day

Clockwise from top left: A kingfisher, a swan, and a cormorant get dinner.

Bird Snacks

Some birds, such as the osprey (below), the seagull (right-hand page, bottom), and hawks, sometimes take part in "flock foraging." In flock foraging, birds search for food in large groups. Biologists have done experiments that prove what these birds must already know: it's better to hunt in a group when there is a lot of prey. When there are just a few prey animals, it's better to hunt alone so you don't have to share.

Great Escape!
A flying osprey carries a fish.

Catch me if you can

Every time an animal goes searching for food, it takes a risk that it might become dinner for a hungry predator. At left, an owl has a vole. At right, a goshawk has a bird. Below, seagulls have caught a starfish (left) and a crab (right).

Seafood Buffet

Bird Snacks

Like most animals, birds have developed some cool adaptations to help them catch food. The pelican below, for example, has a large, stretchy throat pouch. Pelicans use their pouch like a fishnet, diving into a school of fish with their mouth open. When they return to the surface, they lift up their heads so the water drains out, then swallow the fish!

Great Adaptation

A pelican's pouch can hold up to three gallons of water and many fish.

Chow time

This lava heron (left) has a fish in its beak and uses extra-wide feet for wading. An African cattle egret (right) holds a scorpion.

Grocery Bag

How can a puffin hold so many wiggling, slippery fish? Puffins have spines on their tongues that hold the fish in place. This adaptation lets them catch lots of fish at one time.

Jellyfish Snacks

You might need a microscope — or at least a magnifying glass — to see a jellyfish's favorite foods. Jellyfish eat eggs and tiny larvae from fish and other animals that float in plankton. They catch their prey by stinging it with special cells on their tentacles. A few species of jellyfish grow very large and can eat big fish.

Going My Way?

Some types of fish are immune to jellyfish stings. They swim near the jellies, eating leftover food scraps and hiding from predators and prey.

Do you like your eggs scrambled or over easy?

Jellyfish biologists say some types of jellyfish can eat more than 2,000 fish eggs in one day.

Jellyfish Have Predators, Too

Some types of fish, turtles, and nudibranchs eat jellyfish.

Fish Snacks

Underwater animals have some amazing ways to find and catch food. The fish below, called a sarcastic fringehead, makes its home in empty seashells. When small shrimp and crabs come near, this sit-and-wait predator darts out to catch them.

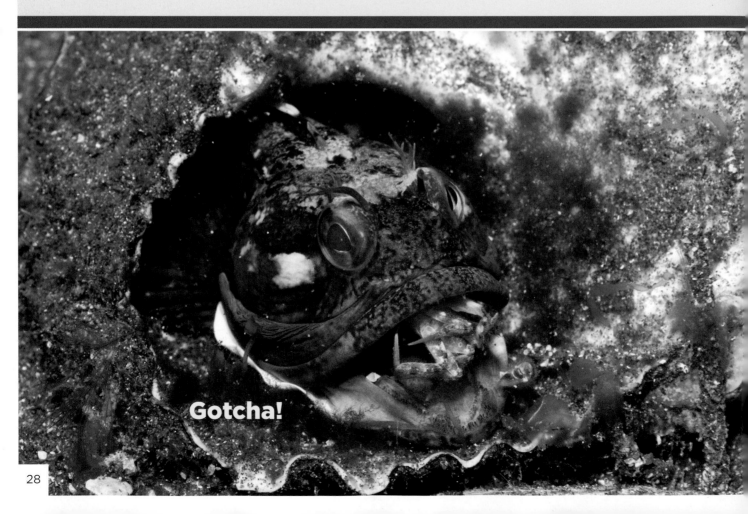

Gotcha!

Treasure hunt

Goatfish (left and below) use their barbells (whisker-like tentacles) to help them find food. The goatfish at left is sifting through sand on the ocean floor to find small worms, mollusks, and crustaceans. Most types of goatfish hunt at night, but the species below hunts in the day.

Fish Snacks

Sometimes, animals have to eat things they don't like to get to the foods they do like. Parrotfish (below left) use their strong, beak-like jaws to chew through rock-like coral while they feed on algae living inside the coral. The coral pieces pass through the fish's digestive system with their waste and become beach sand. Biologists say that just one parrotfish can make a ton of sand every year.

Crunch and Munch

My, what big teeth you have, Grandma!

The wolf-eel (right) is a type of wolf fish, not a true eel. Like the eels below, though, it hides its long, slender body during the day and hunts at night. Wolf-eels feast on snails, crabs, sea urchins, and clams.

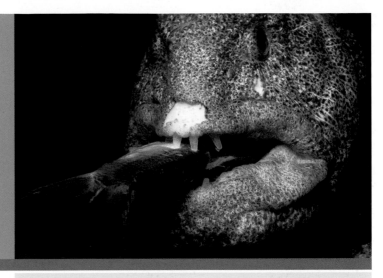

Moray eel The moray eel (left) uses a second set of jaws that have sharp, curved teeth to pull food down their throats. They feed on fish, crabs, and octopus.

Left: Triggerfish have super-strong jaws that allow it to crush and eat animals such as sea urchins, sand dollars, shrimp, crabs, and sea stars. Biologists have watched triggerfish pick up and drop sea urchins and sand dollars over and over until they land upside down. Then, the triggerfish crush their centers and suck out the soft tissue inside.

Mediterranean moray This type of eel (above) lives in holes and crevices in rocky coral reefs. It sleeps during the day and hunts for squid, fish, and crabs at night.

31

Shrimp Snacks

Cleaning stations are special places, usually in coral reefs, where grouper, triggerfish, sharks, rays, and turtles come to be "cleaned" by animals such as cleaning shrimp and cleaner wrasse. The cleaners get a meal of dead and diseased skin, bacteria, and leftover food scraps, while the animals being cleaned get healthier gills and skin. Cleaning shrimp also clean coral and sponges to get food.

Yummy!
Cleaner shrimp dine on a spotted grouper (left) and an eel (right). The eel also has cleaner fish feeding on him.

Trick or treat?

Why doesn't this fish bite down on the cleaning wrasse fish in its mouth? Wouldn't it be an easy meal? Behavior is decided by genes. Fish with genes that cause them to eat their cleaners die sooner from diseases caused by dirty scales and gills, and those genes die with the sick fish. Fish that don't eat their cleaners live longer and leave more offspring with "don't-eat-your cleaners" genes.

Starfish Snacks

Whenever you see a cool underwater animal, look for adaptations that help it get food. To eat a sea urchin, a starfish wraps its legs around the urchin (below), then dissolves the sea urchin's outer shell with its stomach acid and eats the soft meat inside. The starfish (below left) eats small animals that make up sponges and coral by turning its stomach inside out through its mouth.

Lots of Legs

Pinchers come in handy A crab's pinchers are used for defense, attracting mates, and feeding. Above left: A seashore crab scavenges on a dead crab floating near the water's edge. Above right: A coral crab feeds on an anemone. Coral crabs also eat reef sponges.

Underwater snails Nudibranchs are colorful sea slugs that eat jellyfish, coral, barnacles, and sponges (above). They also eat sea squirts (left), a type of animal that lives in groups in oceans. Nudibranchs use tentacles on top of their heads to help them find food.

Sea Squirt Buffet

35

Squid Snacks

Squid use their excellent vision to find prey such as fish and shrimp, then shoot forward using jet propulsion. With eight sucker-lined arms, two front tentacles, and sharp, bird-like beaks, squid are good hunters. When squid are out hunting for fish and shrimp, sperm whales, sea lions, and some birds are out hunting for squid. Marine biologists estimate that sperm males eat more than 400 million tons of squid every year — that's a lot of squid!

Caught in the Act!

The back end of a perch fish hangs out of a squid's mouth.

Ray snacks

Stingrays search ocean floors for crabs, shrimp, worms, and mollusks during high tide. When the tide goes out and the water is shallow, most stingrays stop hunting and hide.

Big Mouth

The manta ray's large, open mouth may look scary, but mantas feed on microscopic animals in plankton, not people!

Whale Snacks

Baleen whales use long plates that grow from the gums in their jaws to filter small fish and microscopic animals in plankton from the water. Some baleen whales have several hundred baleen plates on each side of their mouths! These plates are made from keratin, the material your fingernails are made from. There are 11 species (types) of whales with baleens and most of them are endangered.

Filter Feeder

Dugong & Manatee Snacks

Underwater grazers

Dugongs (left and below) and manatees (right) are large mammals that live in parts of Africa, Australia, Egypt, Belize, and the United States. They are also called sea cows, and are related to elephants.

Take a Deep Breath . . .

Dugongs and manatees eat underwater plants. They can hold their breath for more than five minutes!

Mammal Snacks

Many animals eat more than one type of food. Otters, for example, are known for eating fish (below left), but they also eat crabs (below right), mussels, frogs, eggs, and small mammals, depending on where they live, and which types of animals live near them.

Sushi Snacks

Bark breakfast

Here's your snack quiz question for the day: What can beavers do that most animals can't? Any guesses? Answer: They can eat and digest tree bark! Beavers also eat twigs, leaves, and roots. Like porcupines (below), beavers are a type of rodent, which means their front teeth never stop growing, so they have to chew on a lot of hard things to wear down their teeth.

Take Your Vitamins

Porcupines eat leaves, roots, and the soft plant tissue just under tree bark. They also eat moose and deer antlers to get nutrients such as calcium, phosphorus, and protein.

Mammal Snacks

Animals that eat just one type of food are known as specialists. The giant panda (below) is an herbivore specialist that only eats bamboo plants. An adult panda can eat up to 80 pounds of bamboo a day — that's like you eating more than 2,000 salads! Being a specialist can be a problem if something happens to your one food source, or if lots of animals want the same food.

Picky
Eaters!

Munching marsupials

Kangaroos (left and right) and koala bears (below) are marsupial mammals from Australia. Koalas eat only eucalyptus leaves, while kangaroos eat many types of plants. When biologists did experiments to find out more about kangaroos, they learned that kangaroos do not like to eat plants that are too bitter or too salty.

Mammal Snacks

Animals that eat a lot of fruit are called frugivores. Orangutans (below) are frugivores that also eat leaves and nuts. Orangutans spread fruit seeds as they travel from tree to tree in the forests of Borneo and Sumatra. The savanna baboon (bottom left, right-hand page) live in Africa. These baboons are omnivores, eating leaves, fruits, mushrooms, and small animals.

Tufted capuchin   Plants and flowers are a favorite food of the tufted capuchin (above right). They also eat birds, frogs, and insects.

Pigtailed macaque   The pigtailed macaque (above left) is another frugivore.

Rhesus macaque   Like many primates, the rhesus macaque is an omnivore. The young macaque above is eating termites — yum.

Mammal Snacks

How can people know for sure what wild animals eat? Biologists have several ways to find out. In a study of grizzly bears in Canada, 18 bears were tracked with GPS for three years. Biologists collected more than 650 samples of feces (poop), and analyzed it to learn about the bears' diets. The results? The bears had eaten fruits, flowers, carrion, ants, moose, deer, rodents, and even birds!

Who Needs a Fishing Pole?

How do bears catch fish? Some use their paws, others use their mouths. Polar bears go hunting for something much larger than fish — seals!

Hide 'n seek

Large carnivores such as lions, tigers, and bears spend a lot of energy chasing prey. Usually, there are scavengers nearby, waiting for a chance to steal their food. Leopards solve this problem by carrying their fresh-killed prey up a tree. They eat some when they reach a safe branch, and save the rest for later. Leopards can carry more than 1,000 pounds while they're climbing.

Fast Food!

Mammal Snacks

How much time do you spend every day looking for your lunch? Elephants spend up to 18 hours a day searching for twigs, grasses, leaves, roots, twigs, bark, and fruit. Biologists in Southern Africa and India have used GPS tracking collars to find out which plants elephants eat and how far they travel to get them.

Who Needs a Long Neck?

Elephants use their long trunk to reach for and grab plants.

Salty treat

Giraffes lick tree bark to get salt, calcium, or fiber.

Giraffes travel many miles to find their favorite foods, and can spend up to 20 hours a day eating.

Zebras Zebras spend most of their time grazing on grasses. To find enough food, zebra herds often travel great distances Finding drinking water in their native Africa can also force them to travel a lot.

49

Mammal Snacks

People are often afraid of large mammals that have sharp tusks, teeth, horns, and antlers. Many of the largest mammals, though, are vegetarians. They can do a good job defending themselves and fighting for mates, but they only want to eat plants, not people.

Open Wide, Hippopotamus!

A hippo's mouth can be four feet across when opened wide — you could easily fit inside.

Herbivores Vegetarian snackers clockwise from top right: moose in Alaska, rhinos in Africa, and a cape buffalo from Africa.

Mammal Snacks

If you ask an adult to name three wild mammals, you will probably hear famous animals such as lions, tigers, and bears as answers. There are many other types of mammals, though. The wolverine (right-hand page, top left), for instance, is the largest member of the weasel family, and eats roots, berries, and other mammals. The Tasmanian devil (right-hand page, top right) is a marsupial that eats small mammals and carrion.

Tree-Top Hunter

Foxes, like their close relatives wolves and coyotes, are good hunters. Sometimes they even climb trees to search for food.

Foxes are omnivores, and eat small mammals such as the squirrel shown here, as well as birds, insects, berries, and grasses, depending on the time of year and where they live.

Foxes hide extra food under leaves, snow, and dirt.

Hyenas Known as ferocious scavengers, hyenas (left) often steal the fresh-caught kills of African carnivores such as lions, leopards, jaguars, and cheetahs. The hyena at left is carrying a zebra leg, and several vultures are following close behind, waiting for their chance to steal from the hyena.

Badgers Badgers may take the prize for eating the most types of foods. They have been seen eating snakes, turtles, crocodiles, frogs, fish, young birds, bird eggs, insects, honey, foxes, porcupines, leaves, berries, and much more. The badger above has caught a ground squirrel.

53

Mammal Snacks

There are about 4,500 mammals in the world. They live in many different types of places and eat many types of foods. All mammals are endotherms, which means they cannot use the sun's energy to keep their bodies warm the way reptiles do. Instead, mammals use chemical energy from the foods they eat to heat their bodies, so they need to eat a lot of food.

Food Fight!

Fruit bats find food with their keen eyesight and strong sense of smell.

Is a long snout better than a straw?

Spiny anteaters use their long, sensitive noses to find underground insects, then catch them with their long, sticky tongues. Spiny anteaters are also called echidnas. They live in Australia, New Guinea, and Tasmania.

Fruit Snacker

A fruit bat from Kenya (left) and a brush-tailed possum (above) from Australia.

Mammal Snacks

Biologists describe many animals as "opportunistic feeders," which means they eat several different types of foods. Squirrels, for instance (right-hand page, top left and bottom left) are known as opportunistic feeders. They eat fruits, nuts, and seeds. Another small mammal, the prairie dog (right-hand page, center top), also eats a variety of foods, including seeds, roots, and grasses.

No Cheese For Me!

Mice only eat cheese when they sneak into someone's home. In the wild, mice eat berries (left), seeds (below), leaves, roots, and nuts. Sometimes, mice and rats gross people out by eating dog feces!

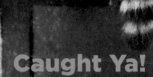

Caught Ya!

Human trash can look like an all-you-can-eat buffet to hungry raccoons.

Top right: A raccoon feasts on a stolen bird egg. Sometimes, raccoons wash their food before eating it.

Mammal Snacks

Mammal moms make milk for their babies. Some newborns nurse for just a few days, while others, such as the elephant, will nurse for years. The milk has a lot of fat in it, which helps newborns build a fat layer in their bodies that will keep them warm. Mammals that live in very cold places have extra fat in their milk. Nursing moms need to eat extra food so their body has enough energy to make the milk.

Drink up!

Adult camels eat grasses and shrubs. A mother camel's milk has a lot of sugar.

Nursing moms Nursing moms clockwise from top right:
A harp seal, African elephant, vervet monkey, and meerkat.

Amphibian Snacks

Amphibians are close relatives of reptiles that live the first part of their lives in the water and their adult lives on land. Amphibians use their eyes to find their food in the daytime, and their sense of smell to find food at night. Salamanders (below) eat spiders, insects, worms, frogs, and other small animals. They also eat the eggs of these animals.

Mouse Trap

A tiger salamander dines on a small mouse.

Gotcha!

Frogs and toads are known for their long, sticky tongues, which help them catch flying insects. At left, a cane toad is eating a katydid.

Bug Bites

When they're adults, frogs eat spiders, insects, small fish, and worms. As tadpoles, they eat algae and microscopic organisms such as bacteria.

Gecko Snacks

Geckos are often described as sit-and-wait predators. They don't have large teeth or claws, like many other carnivores. Instead, they blend in well with leaves and rocks, waiting for prey to come near them. In addition to plant nectar, fruits, and small lizards, geckos also eat many types of insects, including praying mantids, beetles, moths, grasshoppers, termites, and ants.

Sticky Tongues Get More Ants!

A gecko from Madagascar gecko catches ants with its sticky tongue.

Recycle

A single dead gecko can serve as food for thousands of ants.

No water fountains for geckos!

Left: Geckos need water, like all animals. They drink water droplets from rain showers or early-morning dew found on leaves.

Below: The back end of a cricket hangs out of a young leopard gecko's mouth.

Reptile Snacks

Reptiles eat millions and millions of insects. So how can there be any left? You don't need a calculator for this math! Many types of insects can lay hundreds or thousands of eggs at a time, and the newly hatched offspring become egg-laying adults in just a few weeks or months.

Strong Jaws

Broadhead skinks such as this one eat spiders, insects, and other invertebrates. They have very strong jaws, and also eat small mammals or other lizards. Their blue tails may warn predators not to eat them because they will taste bad.

Don't talk with your mouth full!

A chameleon (left) and a bearded dragon (right) eat insects.

Fly Catcher

Chameleons are well adapted for catching flying insects. Their eyes can move in different directions, and their stretchy tongues have sticky tips that bring prey back to their mouths.

Lizard Snacks

Monitor lizards have forked tongues, like snakes, which they use to smell prey. The fork in their tongue tells them which direction to go when hunting. Monitor lizards are the top carnivore in some ecosystems, eating eating mammals, birds, fish, and reptiles.

Take a Deep Breath

Water monitors can hold their breath up to 30 minutes, which helps them hunt under water when they can't find food on land.

A 10-foot dragon? Really?

Komodo dragons (right and below) live on four islands in Indonesia. They are the world's largest lizard, and can grow up to 10 feet long. Komodos are the top carnivore in their homes, and eat large animals such as water buffalo and pigs. They also eat other reptiles, small mammals, and carrion (dead animals).

No Leftovers?

Komodo dragons can eat a lot of food at one time. To kill their prey, komodos inflict deep bites with their sharp teeth. Animals that escape after a bite are followed until the komodo's venom causes blood loss and shock.

Iguana Snacks

Adult black iguanas (below) eat leaves, flowers, and roots. Galapagos land iguanas (bottom right and top left) eat a lot of prickly-pear cactus, which helps them get water into their diet. They even eat the spines! Galapagos marine iguanas (top right) live on land but eat seaweed under water. Iguanas also eat centipedes and insects.

Babies Eat Bugs?

Young iguanas eat insects instead of plants. Biologists who study them think this is because plants are harder to digest.

Ouch!

Turtle Snacks

Turtles and tortoises are herbivores, carnivores, and omnivores, depending on the species and where they live. The carnivores eat small insects and small invertebrates, while the herbivores eat flowers, leaves, bark, and roots. Turtles that spend most of their time in fresh or salt water eat algae, coral, sponges, fish, and even jellyfish.

Flower Power

Many tortoises and turtles eat flowers and flower buds.

Galapagos tortoise snacks

Giant Galapagos tortoises from Ecuador may look fierce, but they are vegetarians, eating grasses, leaves, and cactus. These endangered tortoises have a symbiotic relationship with Galapagos finches. Finches eat insects from the tortoises' necks and shells, which gives the birds a good meal and keeps the tortoises clean. In aquatic turtles and tortoises, cleaner fish eat algae and parasites from the shells. These are called symbiotic relationships because both animals benefit.

Yum, Bubble Coral!

A hawksbill turtle feasts on bubble coral. They also eat coral reef sponges and jellyfish.

Snake Snacks

Snakes eat many types of foods, including birds, amphibians, mammals, and other reptiles. Snakes swallow their foods whole by "walking" their jaws over it. Many people think snakes can eat large animals by unhinging their jaws. Snakes don't actually unhinge their jaws, though. Instead, they have an extra bone between their jawbones and their skulls, and their lower jaw bones are also not attached in the center front, like ours are.

Head First

A tree snake is eating a large lizard with a long tail. Snakes have a very long rib cage, which helps protect their bodies while they eat.

Snakes A rat snake (above) eats a bird egg and a water snake (above left) tackles a fish.

More snakes Frogs are a favorite meal of many snakes. Here, a young green tree python (left) and a water moccasin (above) are eating frogs. Luckily for the world's frogs, most snakes only need to eat once a month!

Crocodile Snacks

Crocodiles and their close relatives, alligators, are often shown eating large animals on television shows. Like all reptiles, crocodiles and alligators are ectotherms, which means their bodies are heated by the sun's energy. Ectotherms do not need to eat as much as animals that use food energy to heat their bodies (endotherms). In fact, research biologists found that a 100-pound dog eats more than an 800-pound alligator!

Fresh Fish!

Ambush Predator

To catch prey, crocodiles often stay very still, with only their well-camouflaged eyes and nostrils on the top surface of the water. When an unsuspecting animal such as this wildebeest comes close, the crocodile rushes forward, jaws open and ready.

Snail Snacks

Many snails eat plants and seeds, but others are carnivores, eating earthworms, slugs, frog eggs, and even other snails. Snails are slow eaters, and can easily become another animal's dinner. A snail's shell helps protect it from predators, but raccoons, birds, and snakes can pull a snail's body out of its shell.

Mushroom Muncher

Above from left to right: Snails use the razor-sharp edges of their tongue (called a radula) to scrape food from algae, a palm seed, and a strawberry.

Left and above: Snails feast on cabbage leaves (left) and frog eggs (above).

Spider Snacks

There are about 38,000 species (types) of spiders, and all are carnivores. Not all spiders catch their prey in webs, though. Some spiders wait for prey to pass by and then ambush them, or chase them down. Male nursery web spiders give their fresh-caught flies to females as mating gifts, all wrapped up in silk. Some males are tricky, giving the females a seed, a bug carcass, or an empty ball of silk instead of a fresh-killed fly!

Gotcha!

Jumping spiders use their many eyes — six or eight, depending on the species — to find flies, then they chase after them and jump on them!

Cool names

The huntsman spider (left) was named for its strong mouth-parts and fast speed, which helps it catch caterpillars, roaches, cockroaches, and other insects. The crab spider, right, was named after its body shape, which looks like a crab. Crab spiders hide inside flowers, catching bees and wasps when they come to feed on flower nectar. Most spiders inject venom into their prey through their fangs.

Dinner to Go!

Tarantulas are nocturnal hunters. They eat snakes, amphibians, insects, and even small birds and mice.

Mantid Snacks

"Praying mantis" is a common name for the mantids, a group of large insects that look like they are praying when they stand still with their front legs folded in front of them. Mantids only look kind, though. In fact, they are fierce carnivores, eating other insects and even small animals such as hummingbirds when they get a chance. Sometimes, but not always, female mantids eat the males after mating.

Built-In Knife

The front legs of mantids are lined with knife-like spines that help rhem hold on to struggling prey, such as this butterfly.

Hide 'n seek

There are almost 2,000 species of mantids. They come in many colors, which help them blend in (camouflage) while they stalk their prey. There's even a pink mantid that hunts and hides in flowers.

Fresh Food

Sharp front legs hold a fresh-caught cricket in place, while strong jaws let a mantid tear off bite-sized pieces.

Butterfly Snacks

Female butterflies lay their eggs in places that have lots of food ready for the newly hatched caterpillars. Caterpillars need to eat lots of leaves to prepare for the time they will spend as a chrysalis, when they will go through metamorphosis, changing into winged adults. As adults, butterflies use their long, hollow tongues like straws to eat fruits and flower nectar.

Trick of the Day:
Eat Without Being Eaten!

Caterpillars are a favorite food of many types of birds, spiders, and other animals. Their colors and patterns often camouflage (blend in) with their environments. Some species have bright colors that warn enemies they taste bad.

Family dinner

You may say YUCK when you learn that these lemon butterflies are eating cow dung, but they aren't the only animals that eat feces. Animals eat poop to get minerals and small pieces of undigested foods.

Upside down dinner If you were a caterpillar, why would you eat upside down? To trick birds, of course! When birds fly overhead, looking down for food, an upside-down caterpillar looks like part of a leaf and not like a treat.

Nectar food A butterfly (left) uses its hollow tongue, called a proboscis, to drink nectar. When they aren't feeding, butterflies keep their tongues rolled up under their chins.

Moth Snacks

Like butterflies, most adult moths eat flower nectar and plant sap, and the caterpillars eat leaves. A few species eat the wool in clothes or the wood in trees, while some others eat grains, fruits, and insects stolen from spider webs. Also like butterflies, moths have hollow, straw-like tongues.

Hummingbird Moths

Hummingbird moths use their super-long tongues to reach nectar deep inside flowers.

Wasp & Bee Snacks

What's wrong with this picture?

Some wasps eat spiders and some spiders eat wasps. The wasp at left is eating a crab spider, while the crab spider on page 79 is eating a wasp! Wasps use their eyesight and sense of smell to find food, such as the dead fish the wasp at right is feasting on.

Pollen Party

Bees spend a lot of energy searching for flowers with pollen and nectar. Scientists who study bees have found that some bees can fly back to their hive carrying 75% of their body weight in food.

Fly Snacks

True flies (below) have just two wings. Several other insects, such as dragonflies, have the word "fly" in their name, but they are not true flies because they have four wings, not two. Flies and dragonflies use their hollow, straw-like tongues the same way moths and butterflies feed. Below, a robber fly (a true fly) eats a small house fly.

Carnivore
Cuisine

Ewwwww . . .

House flies often eat animal feces, which can be moved to the food on your plate if you're not careful.

Above and below Adult dragonflies are generalists, but biologists have noticed they eat a lot of flies (hiding in the flower, above), termites, and beetles (below).

Left and top left Flies feed on many types of food. The fly to the left is feeding on feces, while the fly above left is feasting on flower nectar.

Ant Snacks

There are more than 8,500 species (types) of ants and they live together in large groups. Worker ants search for food, leaving trails with chemicals called pheromones so they can find their way back home. Worker ants carry food back to their nests to feed other members of the group. Most ant species are generalists, which means they will eat any type of food they can find.

Fresh Meat

Snack time

Clockwise from bottom left: Ants eat mushrooms, blueberries, water droplets, bird droppings, and honey-dew from the back end of an aphid. Some species of aphids, such as the one shown bottom right, feed ants, while the ants protect the aphids from predators in a symbiotic relationship.

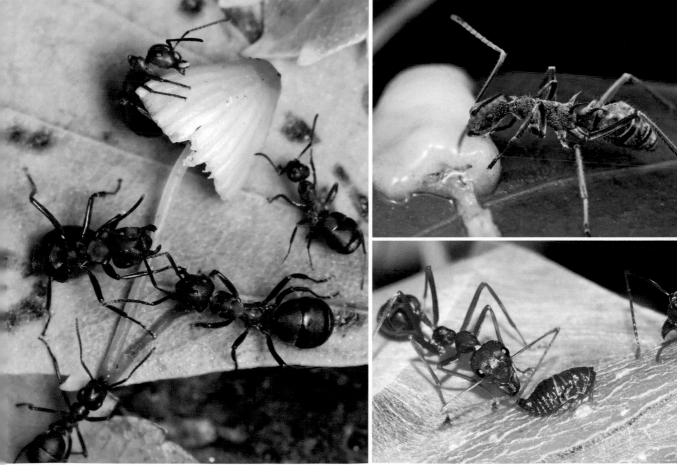

Beetle Snacks

Beetles use their strong jaws to eat many types of foods. The beetle below (left) is a flower beetle, and feeds on nectar and pollen. Beetles also eat small insects and spiders that they find in flower blooms. The weevil below (right) is a type of beetle with a long snout. Weevils eat the soft tissue inside of plants, which makes farmers and gardeners dislike them because they can damage fruits and vegetables.

Flower Feast

Green Salad

Meat eaters

Not all beetles eat plants. The carrion beetle was named for its habit of eating dead animals. The carrion beetle at left is cleaning out a snail shell. At right, a ground beetle feasts on the larva from another insect. Ground beetles also eat snails and worms.

Food names How would you like to be named after your favorite food? How about Pizza Mike or Chocolate Cake Khloe? The insect at left is a potato beetle, and was named for the plant it lives on. Both the larvae and the adults feed on potato plants.

The beetle below is a ladybug in the larval stage, feasting on aphids. Ladybugs are loved by farmers and gardeners because the larvae and the adults eat insects that kill their plants.

Look Inside

Aphid Attack

Scavenger Hunt

Look through the pages of this book to find the items listed below. Use the glossary on the facing page and the index on the next page if you need a little help. When you've finished, study the feeding habits of the animals living near your home and school, then surprise your friends with your own scavenger hunt.

* Find three animals eating spiders.

* Find four animals eating frogs.

* Find three animals eating seeds.

* Find an animal eating a scorpion.

* Find an animal eating a starfish.

* Find a starfish eating an animal.

* Find three animals eating crabs.

* Find five parents feeding their offspring.

* Find three animals eating upside down.

* Find three examples of fructivores.

* Find three animals eating eggs.

* Find three examples of ophiophagy.

* Find two examples of coprophagy.

* Find three examples of herbivores.

* Find three examples of carnivores.

* Find two animals eating bones.

* Find three insectivores.

* Find three animals sharing food.

Glossary

Glossaries are more than just lists of big words that teachers might test you on. They are also great search terms. If you want to learn more about what animals eat, you will have much more success searching with a keyword such as "foraging" than you will searching for a phrase like "how animals find their food."

Adaptation A change in an animal's behavior or anatomy that allows it to compete better.

Ambush Predators A type of predator that hides until prey comes near, then quickly strikes; also called **Sit-and-Wait Predators.**

Carnivores Animals that eat other animals.

Carrion Dead or decaying animals often eaten by scavengers.

Coprophagy Eating feces.

Ectotherms Animals whose body temperatures change with the temperature in the environment.

Endotherms Animals such as birds and mammals that use food energy to keep their bodies warm.

Foraging Searching for food.

Fructivores Animals that feed on fruits.

Generalists Animals that eat many types of foods.

Granivorous Animals that feed on seeds.

Herbivores Animals that eat plants.

Insectivores Animals that feed on insects.

Omnivores Animals that eat both plants and animals.

Ophiophagy Hunting for and eating snakes.

Predators An organism that preys on other organisms.

Prey An animal being hunted or eaten by another animal.

Scavengers Animals that eat dead or dacaying flesh.

Specialists Animals that eat one type of food.

Contributors

The author would like to thank the photographers, biologists, conservationists, universities, museums, zoos, aquariums, and websites listed on these pages for their research, creativity, and dedication to increasing the knowledge base about the organisms in our world.

Images: Abxyz, Alarifoto, Brandon Alms, AMA, John A. Anderson, Anson0618, Costas Anton , ArjaKo, Yuri Arcurs, Evgeniy Ayupov, Abraham Badenhorst, Mike Bauer, Kitch Bain, Geanina Bechea. Dray van Beeck, Dean Bertoncelj, Mircea Bezergheanu, Patrick Bigatel, Bogomaz, Marianne Bones, Mark Bridger, Moritz Buchty, Magdalena Bujak, Stephen Bures, Tom Burlison, Steve Byland, Ziga Camernik, Rich Carey, C. L. Chang, Vitaly Chernyshenko, Ewan Chesser, Circumnavigation, Ant Clausen, Colette3, Cotton Photo, D&D Photos, Sharon Day, Mark Doherty, Dennis Donohue, Dumitrescu, EcovenTures Travel, E-I-E-I-O Fotos, Ekawatchaow, Elenafoxy, Diego Elorza, Dirk Ercken, Evoken, Firelia, FloridaStock, Fotografie, FotoVeto, Four Oaks, Kurt_G, Gelpi, Iliuta Goean, Joe Gough, Ilya D. Gridnev, Arto Hakola, Happystock, Steve Heap, Daniel Hebert, Mark Higgins, Bjorn Hoglund, IDesign, Javarman, Natalie Jean, Matt Jeppson, Kjersti Joergensen, Roger Jones, K. Kaplin, Cathy Keifer, Sergey Khachatryan, Olga Khoroshunova, Heiko Kiera, Kirsanov, Kojik, Hue Chee Kong, Mark Kostich, Kotomiti, Ivan Kuzmin, Eduard Kyslynskyy, Hugh Lansdown, Brian Lasenby, Peter Leahy, Jin Young Lee, David P. Lewis, Don Long, Lumen Digital, Steven Maltby, Steve McWilliam, Roger Meerts, Melissaf84, Vladimir Melnik, MindStorm, Christian Musat, Nagel Photography, Manda Nicholls, Krzysztof Odziomek, Khoroshunova Olga, Sari O'Neal, Monica Ottino, Andrey Pavlov, Michael Pettigrew, Pix2go, Pixel Queen, Sergey Popov V, Paul Prescott, Rattanapat Photo, Radu Razvan, Morley Read, Stefan Redel, Rorem, Scenic Shutterbug, Steve Schlaeger, Thijs Schouten, Richard Seeley, Fedor Selivanov. Galushko Sergey, Uryadnikov Sergey, Graeme Shannon, Misha Shiyanov, Angel Simon, Stefanya, Villiers Steyn, Steffen Foerster Photography, Stubblefield Photography, Mari Swanepoel, Jordan Tan, Nataliya Taratunina, Toa55, Harald Toepfer, Tomo, Mogens Trolle, Undersea Discoveries, Milan Váchal, Vishnevskiy Vasily, Vblinov, Stefanie van der Vinden, Michael Walters, PhD White, Arie V.D. Wolde, Paul S. Wolf, Kim Worrell, Pan Xunbin, Yaroslav, Glenn Young, and 1983paco.

Clockwise starting from top left: A katydid feeds on pollen while grasshoppers feast on leaves and flowers.

Information: AgriLife Extension at Texas A&M, American Wildlife Foundation, Assam Haathi Project, Australian Biological Resources Study, Australian Geographic, Robert P. Bancroft, Colleen Begg, Keith Begg, Cathleen Bester, Mark Boyce, BugGuide.net, Bumblebee.org, Card Wildlife Education Center, Cornell Lab of Orinthology, Cornell University Ask A Scientist, Stephen J.J.F. Davies, Duke University Marine Lab, Earthlife.net, Elephants Without Borders, Fishbase.org, Stephen P. Flemming, Florida Museum of Natural History, Lyn. M. Forster, Malcolm R. Forster, Bryan G. Frya, Georgia Aquarium, Dawn H. Gouge, Monty Graham, Brent M. Graves, Jeffrey Hays, Mary Hoff, Masaki Hoso, Everett Williams Jameson, Josh Justice, Benjamin R. Kovacs, Byron B. Lamont, Mark Malfatti, Marinebio.org, Maryland Cooperative Extension, Rita Mehta, Miinnesota Department of Natural Resources, Robin Munro, Michael H. Parsons, Hans J. Peeters, National Geographic, National Primate Research Cente, NatureWorks, New Hampshire Public Television, Scott Nielsen, Ngorongoro Crater Wildlife, Fritz Obst, Simon Oliver, Carl Olson, Matthew J. Parris, John S. Placyk, M.H. Price, Jose M. Rodriguez, Mark R. Ryan, Jason Sabet-Peyman, Varanus Salvator, Juan José Sanz, Savannah River Ecology Laboratory Herpetology Program, SCIENCE DAILY, Seaworld.org, Seeturtles.org, Norman G. Seymour, Shedd Aquarium, Peter C. Smith, Smithsonian National Zoological Park, Squam Lakes Natural Science Center, Gordon Stenhouse, Michael Stuart, Mari Swanepoel, Wouter Teeuwissed, University of Florida Entomology Department, Matthew D. Venesky, Peter Wainwright, Richard L. Walkup, Richard J. Wassersug, David Wrobel, and Stephen Wroec.

General Index

Organism Index